THE HEALING TRUTH YOU WANT TO KNOW

Other Writings by This Author

There is Nothing But God
and
Understanding God

Absolute Science Practice

THE HEALING TRUTH YOU WANT TO KNOW

Vivian May Williams

The Healing Truth You Want to Know

Mystics of the World First Edition 2018
ISBN-13: 9781946362261
ISBN-10: 1946362263
Published by Mystics of the World

Photography by © Dr. Joel Murphy 2018
www.DrJMphotography.zenfolio.com
Printed by CreateSpace
Available from Amazon.com

Vivian May Williams, 1883–1964
The Healing Truth You Want to Know
    Originally published 1930

Contents

Chapter I
   The Nature of Your True Self 7
Chapter II
   How to Fulfill the Object of Your Life 15
Chapter III
   How Truth Frees You 22
Chapter IV
   Healing Treatments by True Prayer 27
Chapter V
   How to Create through the Power of
   Imagination 37
Chapter VI
   Truth Demonstrations 44
Chapter VII
   Healing Disease and Mental Diagnosis 49
Chapter VIII
   How to Realize Prosperity 56
Chapter IX
   How to See Yourself in Truth 63
Chapter X
   The Basis of Healing 68

About the Author 79

Chapter I

The Nature of Your True Self

In Rev. 10:7 we read, "The mystery of God should be finished." God and His manifestation is no longer any mystery.

His nature, which is the nature of your real Self, is capable of proof when you know how to think rightly. To gain an understanding that will enable you to solve your daily problems, you have to examine the teachings of Jesus Christ. The Principle that he taught two thousand years ago is as available today as it was then and can be demonstrated. Nothing in this relative world has stood the test of time as his words have. He said, "Ye shall know the truth, and the truth shall make you free." This means that we are to know that right "here and now" are we spiritual beings, inheritors of the kingdom; and this knowledge or understanding will set us free from all false beliefs or materiality.

For ages, man has believed that he is a material being subject to sin, disease, and death. It is a misapprehension of existence, absolutely false. There have been many beliefs expressed of and about man, but a practical and demonstrable understanding of Truth is necessary for intelligent, harmonious existence. Mortals will continue to experience inharmony and strive to overcome problems in daily life until they gain an understanding of the real man.

Jesus said, "Ye neither know me, nor my Father; if ye had known me, ye should have known my Father also" (John 8:19). Of whom was he speaking? Certainly many knew Jesus, so to whom did he refer when he said, "Ye neither know me, nor my Father"?

Mind the Primal Cause

God, the Father, is Mind, the primal Cause of all. The "me" to whom Jesus referred is the real man, the image in Mind, the Father. No one has ever seen an idea or image in Mind; therefore, no one has ever seen the real spiritual man, the Son of God.

Jesus is the name of the human, or mortal man, but Jesus never identified himself with the mortal man or the body. He recognized no power separate from Mind, God. By this cognition, he reflected all the powers and aspects of Mind, and these powers and aspects were visibly expressed as a human being performing miracles.

He knew his power to be Mind, so he declared, "If ye had known me, ye should have known my Father (Mind) also."

The Nature of Your True Self

Man is more than a material form with a mind inside. Man as the image and likeness is as infinite as God.

If you have a mortal, finite conception of yourself, you cannot embrace the infinite glories of Life and Love.

A finite conception of man does not satisfy that human craving for better, higher, and holier things.

Since God is Mind, the real man must be an idea, which is the offspring (Son) of Mind (Father).

As humanity gains the true conception of man and God, the human capacities are enlarged and perfected, and we witness men with more God-like powers and aspects. Deducing one's conclusions as to man from the imperfect mortal which we witness through the physical senses, one can no more arrive at the true conception or understanding of man than a sculptor can perfect his outlines while holding in thought an imperfect model. One can never discern the spiritual man by holding a material man in thought.

At this point, the question most naturally arises: "How am I to discern between the spiritual man and the material or human man?" I have just explained the image as the Son, or real, spiritual man. In order to be the image of anything, it must be a representation. Since man is God's image, he must be the full representation of Him; therefore, to understand the qualities and aspects of your real Self, you must contemplate the aspects of

God, realizing that these are your qualities, your real nature. This is revealing the "mystery that was hid from the beginning"—that man is really Godlike.

The Truth about Yourself

This is the truth about yourself, and right here you must learn to stand. You have never seen the real man any more than you have seen God. You can know him, however, by observing the visible expression of Good, God. The real man is Soul, identity, and not the body which we see.

Soul, as individualization, reflects Spirit, God, and the body which we call the human or mortal man is the visible effect of the invisible idea, image, or spiritual man.

Millions have read this statement: "Let us make man in our image, after our likeness" (Gen. 1:26). Webster defines image as "an idea; a conception."

Let us fathom this statement in Genesis. God as Mind is Creator of all. Mind, the primal Cause or Substance, thinks. The culmination of Its thinking is an idea, conception, or image in the Mind Itself. The image (offspring of Mind) most naturally becomes the subject of Its thinking, and so we have spiritual man as God's idea of Himself.

The Nature of Your True Self

How Ideas Become Realities

Man is Mind's idea of Itself; man is God's expression of Himself.

The thought (offspring) of Mind is naturally the Son of God. So we conclude with St. John: "We (spiritual beings) are the Sons (ideas) of the living God (Mind)." As Mind contemplates Its image (Son), this image is externalized, embodied or objectified, and so we have an internal or invisible image and an external or visible embodiment, or body, which is falsely termed material man. If it were not for the body or form which bears evidence to the omnipresence of the image or idea, you would never know God or spiritual man. Everything in the visible universe is an identification of the invisible universe. As St. Paul put it, "The things which are unseen are clearly discerned by the things which are seen."

The objects of Life have no separate life of their own. All life and form we see is the reflection of the one Life. What appears as separate men and women is the objective state of Life, but they have no initiative of their own. The activity, feeling, and form that we witness in any object, including the human body, is not in the body but is the result of an effect of consciousness outside the body which is properly named Soul, Mind, Life.

An artist is not "in" his painting, so you are not "in" your body. Your body is an out-picturing of your Mind. Your body is the visible manifestation or expression of you (the image) in Mind, God. Paul said, "You are hid with Christ (Truth) in God."

The Relation of Mind and Body

An object held before a mirror does not get into the mirror but is reflected by it. Mind, in reflecting Its images, does not become absorbed by them, but Its reflections are identifications of the images. So it is with your body. Your Mind reflects, governs, and controls your body but never enters the body any more than a rose held in front of the mirror can enter the mirror but is perfectly reflected by it. One gains dominion over the body in proportion as he is able to grasp this great truth—that man's Mind is God; therefore, his Mind (God) is free at all times to master the body and all externalizations.

Believing Mind is in the body makes one a slave to body and circumstances. Realizing that Life, Mind, is not in the body is the truth that sets you free.

As one realizes his Mind is God, he has "dominion over the earth." The greater appreciation he gains of his Mind the greater will be his objectification. Instead of continually attempting to improve himself, he will understand that he is now the perfect image in Mind. Holding this conception in Mind, most naturally it must be reflected, and the result will be a happy, harmonious man (manifestation). This understanding of the real man does away with all physical struggling we have all indulged in during our past studies.

To sum up the whole: this body which we have called the material man is the objectification or expression of Soul and Soul is the identity of Spirit. One great metaphysician truly said that God unexpressed "would be a nonentity." So our bodies are the identification of Soul, Spirit, God.

There is no material man. In speaking of the material man, Jesus said, "You were a liar from the beginning." A liar is one who speaks falsely. The material man is a false conception of the real, spiritual man. St. Paul said, "Ye are gods," and "the scripture cannot be broken."

Begin today to rid yourself of material conceptions by identifying yourself with Spirit and not with the body.

Your Body Will Picture Whatever You Believe Yourself to Be

Your body will be a perfect picture of whatever you believe yourself to be. If you believe you are Mind rather than body, you will out-picture in your bodies and affairs all the qualities and aspects of God.

Try to look upon your body as having no more life *of its own* than the man on the moving picture screen. He appears to have life of his own, but it is reflected to him by the Intelligence which operates back of the camera and the negative.

Our bodies appear to have life due to the fact that Intelligence, Life, God, is operating behind the image held in the camera of Mind. As Intelligence reflects Its light (understanding) upon this image (film or negative), these images or reflections are seen as men and women with the mental powers and capacities of God. Now you can readily see why Jesus said he had no life but the life of the Father, no power but the power of God.

"I of mine own self can do nothing."

The understanding of this unity of God and Man is the Christ-Consciousness, the Truth—"the truth that makes you free."

Chapter II

How to Fulfill the Object of Your Life

Buddha said, "Ignorance of truth is the cause of all misery ... come to me and I will teach you the truth and the truth will dispel your sorrows."

This truth that we are to learn is that the kingdom of heaven is here at hand; that everything we ever hope to have or to accomplish is finished.

Right here the student questions, "If this is true, why do I not see it in manifestation?" The answer is quite simple: you are not making the proper conditions in consciousness through which this infinite Mind can express Itself in terms of what we call material things.

For centuries, electricity existed without man's consciousness of it, but when it became a realization, man made the proper conditions through which it might be differentiated in terms of light, heat, and power.

The Part Man Plays in Creation

In order to clear up any misapprehension regarding the part man plays in creation, we will consider briefly the object of life. Just trying to destroy inharmony that we might experience peace does not deliver one, but *insight* does free you because it looks beyond conditions into realities.

To gain an object of life in the material world, we have to consider the object of life in the spiritual world, called heaven. Heaven is God's consciousness.

We will now consider the object of the spiritual man's existence in the world of reality, called heaven. God unexpressed would be a nonentity, so God in Self-contemplation (for there was no manifest thing to contemplate) reflected, or objectified, His own ideas or images; this creation or manifestation is termed man.

As electricity would be unknown without its manifestation, so God would be unknown without man. The two coexist as Mind and idea. God thinks, knows, loves, enjoys, and does all things by means of man. "Thou hast created all things, and for thy pleasure they are and were created" (Rev. 4:11). So you can readily see that the object of creation is to give life, love, wisdom, intelligence, health, wealth, and happiness to His spiritual beings that constitute His consciousness.

How Man Comes to See Truth

As man contemplates the object of creation in this light, he is making the proper condition in consciousness, and then Mind is seen to work by means of man. From this viewpoint, life takes on a new aspect and you no longer struggle for a living—you will know Life *is*.

Until electricity was made manifest, we might say it was "without form and void"—it had no means of expression. Man discovered this great essence of power and furnished various appliances; then the electricity began to exist as light, heat, and power. In the power or essence itself, there is no action, for it just "is" electricity and has no consciousness of such manifestations as curling irons, toasters, heaters, light globes, or dynamos.

There Is Joy in Expression

As an illustration, let us presume the essence of electricity symbolizes Mind, and it could say, "Let us create light, heat, and power in our image." Then let us presume that the light globes, motors, heaters, irons, etc., which are the channels through which the power of electricity flows, were conscious beings. Do you not think they would be joyously happy in expressing the power of electricity through themselves? And would not the power, if it were Mind, God, receive joy and happiness in expressing Itself through the globes, motors, heaters, and various appliances?

This should give you an idea of the part man plays in creation. Man is the activity or expression of God. You can also see that if the electric toaster could speak to the heater, it would say, "I am you and you are me—we are both expressing the same substance of electricity." So it is with human beings.

"Love thy neighbor as thyself" means to see yourself in the other fellow and treat him exactly as you would treat yourself.

Sin and Sickness Disappear
Before the Light of Truth

There is a great deal of talk in metaphysics about using your Principle to overcome sin, disease, and all kinds of limitations. You cannot use Principle, for Principle is God. You do not use your Principle, but your Principle uses *you* as soon as you recognize Its perfection.

As one endeavors to become a witness to all good, he makes the proper connection, and the manifestation naturally follows. When you want light made manifest, you furnish the power of electricity with a light globe. Do you have to worry as to how the power operates to give you light? Not for an instant.

Your thoughts stand in the same relation to Mind, God, as the light globe stands to electricity. If you desire health, give that idea to the power, and if you do not direct the power by negative thoughts, you shall manifest health. So it is with anything you may desire.

How to Fulfil the Object of Your Life

How You Fulfill the Law of Life

Endeavoring to understand the object of creation places you in conscious communication with God, which is equivalent to contacting the power of electricity through the medium of a light globe, an idea used to manifest power in terms of light. One fulfills the laws of life as he strives to realize spiritual things. St. Paul said, "The things which are not seen" are clearly discerned by "the things which are seen."

Learn to appreciate every object in this world as bearing evidence to a spiritual idea, and you will soon lose all false concepts of a material universe and see the "new heaven and the new earth" here and now.

Since God had a definite purpose in creating man, or the universe, so you must have a definite purpose in everything you attempt to manifest. You do not have to concern yourself about Mind and Its ways and means of working, but you do have to be greatly concerned about the thoughts you furnish your mind to work upon. If you desire to vacuum clean your rugs, you would not apply a coffee percolator to the electricity, would you? If you desire prosperity and continue to complain of poverty, it will be as impossible to attain wealth as it would be for one to expect to clean his rugs with the coffee percolator.

Mind is impressionable, plastic. Its nature is to give—in giving, it naturally receives. "Ye ask and receive not, because ye ask amiss." You talk disease and expect health; talk poverty and wonder why God does not shower you with abundance.

*Constructive Thought
Brings Demonstration of Truth*

God's work is finished. It is up to man to apply constructive thoughts and exercise the dominion that is his divine birthright. Let us take for granted that the kingdom of heaven is finished and complete—that every good and perfect gift already exists, although unseen, as the apostle James said.

The kingdom of heaven is the world of reality, a world wherein are no limitations and no consciousness of evil. It is a perfect state of mind, established from the beginning. It is God—with no object but love for His spiritual beings.

God finished His work and saw that it was very good, but "a mist went up from the earth." What is this mist that seems responsible for all of man's troubles? Since heaven is God's consciousness, evil cannot enter there to disturb man, so what causes all this inharmony?

Suppose you draw upon your imagination to the extent that you can see the spiritual world with its spiritual beings governed and controlled only by God. Then suddenly a curtain or a veil is drawn in front of it. This veil would be like a mist—occasionally thinning away so you could actually observe the beauty, joy, and happiness of the spiritual world; then again, the mist might become so dense that you could not catch even the faintest glimpse of heaven, and you could observe nothing but the curtain or mist.

Bear in mind the fact that heaven is a perfect state wherein is all joy, happiness, health, wealth, and beauty. The curtain or "veil that is spread over all nations" (Isa. 25:7) is a mist of ignorance or false thinking which, when indulged in, hides the beauty and harmony of our perfect state of mind called heaven.

How is one to get rid of this veil of misery and enter into heaven? By contemplating the perfection of the spiritual world, the action of God which is always taking place upon man, this mist is dispelled and man witnesses heaven. As this action takes place, dispelling wrong thoughts, man awakens in consciousness to find himself in the kingdom of heaven (harmony) here and now, thus fulfilling the scriptural saying, "Thy kingdom come … in earth, as it is in heaven."

Chapter III

How Truth Frees You

The question that is asked me more frequently than any other is: "What is evil, and what is its origin?" In order to answer such questions, we have to reason from a scientific basis.

To begin with, we all admit God to be the only power and that power to be infinite good. "In the beginning was the Word, and the Word was with God, and the Word was God" (John 1:1). Let us examine this statement from the basis of absolute truth.

A word is an audible expression of thought. One cannot express thoughts or words without Mind, so we take it to mean that "in the beginning the Word," or right thought, was the primal power.

The next statement is: "And the Word was with God." In other words, the Word, or right thoughts, are in Mind, or with God.

"And the Word was God" means that right thoughts and Mind (God) are one and the same.

"The same was in the beginning with God." In other words, Mind and right thinking have eternally coexisted.

"All things were made by him" means that everything God, the good true Word, or thought, created is permanent, indestructible—the truth.

"And without him was not anything made that was made." This latter statement is the solution to the question "What is evil?"

Evil claims to have existence, to have as great a power as good, but everything that was not created by God *was never created*—therefore is nothing. Then where does evil get its origin? Since God is the source of all, and that all is good, then evil has no origin. To have an origin, a thing must have permanence, reality. The very fact that evil disappears in the light of truth proves its non-reality. Evil has but a *seeming* existence, and when you understand its nothingness, the illusion disappears and you demonstrate the allness of God, good.

In our present state of consciousness, many things have the semblance of being real but are, according to Truth, merely the manifestation of erring, illusory thoughts. These erring thoughts were not "made by him"; consequently they are not real. John evidently knew that evil thoughts, as well as right thoughts, were objectified, and he differentiated between the two by saying "the Word (right thought) was God," and anything that He did not make was never made. If a thing was never made, it has no life or existence, hence is nothing at all.

Now, if evil is "nothing," why struggle to release yourselves from nothing? Jesus spoke of evil as a murderer from the beginning and having no truth in him; therefore, evil of every nature, even though it is plainly visible to the senses, is never real and at best is but a false sense.

Right thought (Word) was never created—it always existed with God. Evil, being a false belief in the absence of good, is dependent upon good for its existence; hence, it had a beginning and must end.

Life Is Light

"And the life was the light of men." Right thinking, or our consciousness of God, is our life, or mental light. Light is understanding, or spiritual consciousness.

"The light shineth in darkness" means that even though we are in mental darkness, or ignorance, the light, truth, is ever shining in consciousness, and a recognition of this truth is man's sure deliverance from the false conception of evil.

At one time there was a belief that the Earth was flat, and the mediaeval church burned those who denied the so-called fact. Who created the flat Earth? It never existed. For a thing to have existence, it must have permanence, and having permanence it has reality and is indestructible. It was proved to be an illusion, a lie about the round Earth, when Columbus sailed around it.

Was the flat Earth changed into a round Earth by Columbus' discovery? No, because the flat Earth never existed in reality. It was but a false concept in the mind of man. When the truth about the Earth being a sphere was revealed, the flat Earth, or lie, disappeared. So a belief in a material world with all its misery is as much an illusion as the flat Earth. As you learn the truth about yourself, the lie or illusion is dispelled and you catch a glimpse of heaven here and now.

Evil is only a temporary false sense, and when you know the truth about it, it disappears even to the finite human senses.

As far as you are concerned, your thought of a thing is all there is of the thing. What we do is form concepts of and about the things we see around us, and our concepts are not always true. "Now we see through a glass, darkly."

Many persons believe that evil conditions strengthen them and that God intends them to suffer in order to gain good. This is absolutely false, for it is equivalent to saying God knows evil. Good and evil cannot mix any more than oil and water. Such beliefs place man in bondage to material laws. Your divine heritage is good—first, last, and always—and if you experience an evil condition, whether it is physical, financial, domestic, or otherwise, it is due to ignorance of the laws of right thinking.

The Healing Truth You Want to Know

How Truth Will Free You

It will be seen, therefore, that what we want for freedom is knowledge of Truth, an understanding of God.

Chapter IV

Healing Treatments by True Prayer

Treatment is the word used to indicate that form of prayer or right thinking which is based upon absolute good. The theologian calls it thinking of God and heaven; the scientific men refer to it as cause and its manifestation; the metaphysicians, Mind and Its ideas. The word *treatment* signifies the line of demarcation between prayer based upon a scientific principle and supplicatory prayers offered to a distant potentate, who may or may not hear, or even answer, the pleading supplicant.

Treatment is true prayer, conscious communion with God. You will note that I said *conscious* communion with God, for some believe that all that is necessary to bring about harmonious results is to take a few constructive affirmations and repeat them over and over. This sort of treatment may easily become "sounding brass and a tinkling cymbal," the very thing Jesus warned mankind against. It is *conscious realization*, based on scientific facts about God and man, that brings about your demonstrations.

Jesus Christ gave his healing instruction in a very few words. He said, "Ye shall know the truth, and the truth shall make you free." There is no responsibility whatever placed upon anyone except to "know the truth"—God does the work.

An Almost Instantaneous Healing of Quinsy Sore Throat

Many years ago, I had proof of the simplicity of treatment and realized once and for all exactly what the Master meant when he said, "Ye shall know the truth, and the truth shall make you free."

I was walking through a field and came upon a strange man at work. I spoke to him, and during our conversation he told me he was suffering from quinsy and that his physician told him he could expect no relief for five days.

The instant he said "quinsy," that statement of Jesus rang in my ears, and along with it came a glorious realization of the fact of the perfection of this man in God's image instead of seeing him as a material man to be healed of quinsy. I wasted no time thinking how to heal him by long prayers, but obeyed the inner voice that seemed to say, "All you need to do is to turn to God and know the perfection of His man, and the Truth (Christ) will set him free." All the while he talked to me, I was silently reversing false thoughts by contemplating the spiritual man in all his glory. Then I turned and went on my way.

In about an hour I passed again, and he asked me what I had done to him when I first met him. I had to force myself to even recall the incident, for it was completely erased from my consciousness. Suddenly, I recalled the statement he made about his suffering, and I told him I knew the truth for him. My words seemed to convey no meaning to him, so I went on to explain how utterly impossible it is for an image to be unlike the original, and told him since God did not have quinsy, he, being God's image, could not have it—this is absolute truth. He went on to tell me that ten minutes after our first conversation he discovered his throat was perfectly healed.

*Healing Is Only a
Change in Consciousness*

I did not change quinsy into health; neither did God create new health for him. God's creation is finished, and His spiritual man is eternally healthy. I became conscious of the spiritual man's harmony (the truth), and the Truth being Christ, this man was set free by means of the Christ. Paul said, "I do all things through the Christ."

You may wonder how my consciousness could affect the other fellow. There is but one subconscious mind. If I drive false thoughts out of my consciousness with the intention of helping another, the one to whom I direct my thoughts will get the help, for the other fellow is my concept.

This is "casting the beam out of thine own eye so thou canst see clearly to cast the mote out of thy brother's eye."

Out duty is to reverse every thought that is unlike God and to do it without any consideration of personal compensation. When you find yourself thinking of health, it is a sign health is established for you. You would never desire a thing if something did not tell you it was somewhere present for you.

Thoughts are like signposts pointing the way to either heaven or hell, for we make our own comparative heaven and hell by the way we think.

Your thoughts are like a weathervane. When the weathervane points to the South, it does not cause the south wind to blow, but it is a sign that the south wind is blowing. When you find yourself treating for health, it is a sign that the action of your perfect health, "hid with Christ in God," is causing your thoughts to turn to it in recognition. Your thoughts, like the weathervane, point to the source of activity.

The Basis of All Healing Treatment

There are numerous methods of healing, and results are obtained through the practice of each, the reason for this being that Mind, Consciousness, is the basis of all treatment. "As a man thinketh, so is he." The woman who believed she would be healed if she touched the hem of Christ's garment functioned her belief. Jesus said to her, "Thy faith has made thee whole." He did not say he healed her.

Denials and affirmations are very effective in treatment, provided you realize the truth back of the statements rather than laying stress upon mere words. Unless you put feeling into your statements, you will continue indefinitely and wonder why your affirmations do not work.

It is a mistake to depend upon any fixed formula in truth. In attempting to use any method of treatment, you will be inclined to wonder what the words mean rather than getting away in thought from the material world to heaven and thinking of God.

Too much stress is laid upon the conception of treatment in the metaphysical field today. Many believe they have to be continually treating against conditions and circumstances in order to exist. Get out of the old habit of thinking everything needs treatment, for entertaining such false beliefs keeps up a continuation of old conditions that will eternally need a treatment.

Instead of taking the attitude that you have something to get rid of, turn in thought to God and the world of reality, and know there are no evil conditions to overcome.

The Healing Truth You Want to Know

Suggestions to Beginners in Truth Study

If you are a beginner and find it difficult to forget conditions and circumstances, here are a few suggestions to assist you. Do not use them as a formula—let God lead you. In taking up treatment for any specific thing, remember that the same principle applies to all. Until you are sufficiently advanced to know there is nothing to treat (this being the highest form of treatment), it is best to take each specific problem, deny its existence in the world of reality and affirm the completion of the thing desired.

Put life, feeling, and joy into your treatments—words avail you nothing unless they are animated by your spirit or realization.

Suppose you were in financial difficulty and desired to free yourself. Turn in though to God. Deny that there is any material man to be in trouble or to lack, and realize the abundance of the spiritual man. Allow your thoughts to dwell upon the thing as you desire it in completion. Emerson said, "Assume the virtue, and you shall have the realization." Assume that the thing you desire exists now in the world of reality that is all around us. *Let your treatment be one of glorious realization of the truth about God rather than a striving to overcome difficulties.*

Healing Treatments by True Prayer

You Should Not be Concerned about Results

You do not have to be the least bit concerned about the results, for that is God's business. Treatment, or true prayer, is the active, conscious thinking that harmonizes you with the world of reality, wherein every demonstration you ever hope to make is already accomplished. The apostle James said that the "good and perfect gift" already exists, although unseen. You cannot create health, wealth, or prosperity through thinking, but right thinking (treatment) enables you to become *conscious* of the health, wealth, and prosperity eternally established in the invisible world. You are not saved by words but by virtue of *what you are*—God's image.

A question that frequently arises is: "Can I treat for anyone without his consent?" When you treat, it should be clearly understood that you are the person for whom, in the first instance, the error has to be destroyed. When the false belief in the disease or trouble that appears is thoroughly destroyed in your own consciousness, and the truth is realized of the perfection of man as God's image, then it is that the patient is freed. All there is to any trouble is your concept of it. Reverse your thoughts, and you are free.

"How am I to handle evil conditions?" Since evil is darkness, ignorance, illusion, nothingness, there is no way to destroy "nothing" except by knowing its nothingness. The student usually admits evil as something, then sets to work to destroy "something" which he declares is nothing, thus carrying on a war in his own consciousness.

Jesus said, "I came not to destroy but to fulfill." Denials tear down—they attempt to destroy. Insight is fulfillment, for it looks through evil conditions into reality. When one looks through to reality, he does not attempt to destroy the evil he admits is present, but he denies that it has any reality of its own, any permanent existence, since God (Good) fills all space. Evil is present only as an illusion in human consciousness, just as a shadow creates the illusion that the sun is not shining.

If it were not for the false sense that mortals entertain, instruction would not be necessary. The false sense needs to be educated. As one loses the false sense of limitation, the perfection which was always established becomes visible to the senses.

The Illusion of Evil

This illusion of evil can well be illustrated by the sleeping dream. One great metaphysician has said:

> The history of error is a dream-narrative. The dream has no reality, no intelligence, no mind; therefore the dreamer and dream are one, for neither is true nor real (Mary Baker Eddy).

In your sleeping dream, you may take on the characteristics of another person, or you may dream that you are away from home and in great trouble. Although your mind experiences this dream, you are still but one person—the man in bed. The person away from home and in trouble was an imaginary man in your own mind. When you awoke, he only *seemed* to disappear, for he really was not there. The only existence he had was in your dream state.

Your waking experience is in identically the same dream state. Although you are a spiritual being in heaven, governed and controlled by God, you are believing you are a material man in a material world liable to sin, disease, and death. Struggling to free yourself from evil through cut and dried methods and systems of thought is equivalent to trying to free yourself from some condition in your dream when you are really not in it.

How to Stop the Seeming Dream of Evil

If you could be conscious of the fact that you were only dreaming when you were experiencing an unpleasant dream, all you would have to do to end the experience would be to become conscious of the truth about yourself—that is, that the dream was taking place in your own mind—and your dream would cease.

This same applies to our waking state. In order to stop this seeming dream of evil, one must continually tell himself he is a spiritual being, governed and controlled only by God, right here and now. One awakens himself out of the false sense of evil by understanding that he is in the world of reality now. This is Absolute Truth—"the truth that makes you free."

A dream could not exist without someone to dream it. The material world, with all of its evil beliefs, will cease to exist when man ceases to believe evil is real. Disease is a false belief about health. Poverty is a false belief in the absence of wealth. Destroy the beliefs and you experience the omnipresence of health and wealth.

Darkness is not real—it is but the absence of light. When the light enters the room, the darkness does not leave. You do not have to destroy evil—the illusion disappears when you realize the truth about God and man.

"Before they call, I will answer." Before you call for health, wealth, and success, you are answered, for the finished kingdom is at hand. In the midst of the greatest problem is your answer—God's omnipresence. Understanding, perception, and vision are man's only redemption.

Chapter V

How to Create through the Power of Imagination

"He is a rich man who can avail himself of all men's faculties" (Emerson). There is one faculty of man that has been sadly neglected and which can be traced back to a fundamental principle and found to be the greatest faculty he possesses. In fact, it is the creator of the universe. Man's recognition of this great faculty within reach of his own conscious thinking gives him dominion over the earth.

It is the realization of this great truth that links man up with the Divine. Everything in the manifest world is in subjection to the power of the imagination.

Let us take the Bible for an authority and turn to the first chapter of Genesis, where we read, "God created man in his own image, in the image of God created he him." Webster defines image: "To form an image of; to portray to the mental vision; a picture produced by reflection."

How Mind Creates

Since nothing could possibly exist prior to Mind or consciousness to conceive it, it is only logical to presume that man is the natural out-picturing or manifestation of an image held in Mind. An image can only dwell in the imagination, which is the productive or creative faculty of mind. So the heavens and the earth were formed through constructive images or ideals held in Mind.

Some people may confuse fancy with imagination, for both fancy and imagination recombine and modify mental images;. The one great distinction between them is that fancy is superficial, while imagination is deep, essential, spiritual. Fancy flits about the surface and is airy and playful, sometimes petty and sometimes false; imagination goes to the heart of things and is deep, earnest, serious, and seeks always and everywhere for the truth.

The imagination of man is the window or door which, when thrown open by knowledge of scientific thinking, lets the divine Life stream into his life. It is the imagination that enables man to transcend relative thinking; to release himself from the bondage of old conditions and put on the new. Through the imagination, man is brought into a condition of consciousness which is called inspiration, and this state of mind enables him to conceive new ideas. Inspiration links man with his Creator, Mind, and brings into existence our poets, composers, prophets, seers, mystics, and all great inventors.

How to Create through the Power of Imagination

This process of creative thinking is used unconsciously by many, for it is the natural birthright of man. The man who is fortunate enough to realize its great power sufficiently to use it consciously is the man who can transform his life and affairs at will. The great mistake that almost everyone makes in working out his problems is that he depends upon a power separate and apart from himself.

The nature of mind is to function or objectify every image, idea, or thought impressed upon it. If you regard the power as separate from yourself, that will be your idea, and your mind will oblige you by expressing exactly the idea you give it. You will be eternally looking to some unseen power or force to deliver you rather than depending upon your own intelligence, which is always available to assist you.

Mind is like a mirror—a perfect reflector. It works deductively and needs no assistance whatsoever in working out any idea, once it is given a perfect image or blueprint.

How Your Mind Mirror Works

Liken your mind unto a mirror; your thoughts are the images or objects you place before it. If you hold thoughts of disease before your mental mirror, your reflection will be one of disease.

Suppose you do not like the reflection and want to rid yourself of it. Would you quarrel with the mirror for reflecting it? Would you still hold the disease thoughts before it and then decide to deny and affirm until the condition disappeared, or would you remove the objects or images before the mirror? As long as any thought is held in mind, it will continue to be objectified according to your mental conviction of it.

It was the use of the imagination that enabled Jesus Christ to look into reality and see life in the place of death; to see abundance, instead of lack; to break down the seeming laws of materiality. Where did our radios, airplanes, wireless, and all other inventions originate but in that great creative power of man—his imagination? No one has ever seen an idea, but everything in this world bears evidence to an idea in mind.

*Success Is Founded Upon
the Individual's Imaging Power*

Anyone who has achieved unusual success has done so through this great unseen quality of mind, rather than depending upon that which is already made manifest. The source and center of man's creative power that lifts him above the level of brute creation, that gives him power to transcend all relativity, is his power of imagination. You must have a definite purpose in mind—a complete idea of the thing desired.

Since mind is the basis of your being, you do not have to instruct it as to *how* you think the

How to Create through the Power of Imagination

demonstration should come about, but your duty is to give it as perfect an image or idea as you desire made manifest. When you have done this, the next great step toward fulfillment is to create the *feeling* you would experience if you were in actual possession of your ideal.

Can you imagine an artist being a success if he did not put *feeling* into his images? St. John said, "Love is the fulfilling of the law." Love symbolizes the female element of mind, whereas, reason is the symbol of the male. When we link up logical reason (the male element) with love or feeling (female), we have a perfect creation or demonstration of mind.

An image in mind is a spiritual reality—the offspring of Mind, Mind's subject or son. As Mind contemplates Its image, or son, it becomes man, or manifestation. So it is with man as God's image.

The same process goes on in man's thinking. His mind is his creator, his images or ideas are his offspring or son, and as he contemplates his own ideas they become his manifestation. *Mind has the power to manifest any idea man conceives.* Man is limited only by his inability to conceive constructive ideas.

If false thoughts keep one in bondage, then he needs something besides thinking to remove the burden. That which transcends thinking is the imagination, which arrives at the point of conviction without the reasoning process.

Jesus Used Imagination Constantly

Jesus taught in parables—drew imaginary pictures—because he knew the minds of the people could grasp a picture or image much more readily than they could reason.

When you look at a painting, instantly your mind grasps the whole idea before you have time to think of details or begin to reason. Many fail to demonstrate because they allow reason to prevent them from holding the clear image in the mind until it is objectified.

Ideas are spiritual realities, and when you conceive an idea for good, you have received the actual thing. Jesus gave thanks before he saw the manifestation, for he knew he was mind (not body) and that ideas are realities to consciousness. Here is where the imagination plays the important part. When you are witnessing an imperfect manifestation and desire to change it, you cannot do it while it is evident to the senses. That which enables you to transcend the five physical senses is the imagination.

The Imaging Power in Healing

Every practitioner who ever healed a disease did it through the power of a perfect image held in the imagination. If I tell you to turn in thought to God and heaven, and realize the spiritual man as being healthy, wealthy, and prosperous, do you not use your imagination? You must, for eye has never seen God, heaven, nor the spiritual man.

Some argue that it is wrong to image. Could an artist paint a picture without holding an image in mind? Can you think of a single thing without associating form with it? Form is an idea in Mind, and without it we would have no objects.

> When thou prayest (desire is prayer), enter into thy closet (consciousness), and when thou hast shut thy door (turned away from material beliefs), pray to thy Father (Mind) which is in secret; and thy Father (your Mind) which seeth in secret (beholds an image or picture) shall reward thee openly (shall be objectified, become visible) (Matt. 6:6).

Chapter VI

Truth Demonstrations

We hear a great deal about the word *demonstration*, but few seem to realize its full meaning.

Webster defines demonstration: "to prove so conclusively your side of the question that the other side looks ridiculous." To make a demonstration, you prove the truth of Life so conclusively to yourself or your patient that any opinion to the contrary would seem ridiculous.

Several years ago, I was with a friend who was suffering from a bunion. Not knowing how to reverse his own thoughts, he continually reminded me and the whole household of the discomfort he was experiencing from his bunion. I made no reply for several moments, for I was trying to clear my own thoughts about his condition, and I could not do this until I was able to transcend his negative statements.

Finally, I realized the truth, and the next time he complained, I said, "I am tired of hearing you tell lies about yourself." This startled him (just what I intended), for he believed he was telling the truth when he said he had a bunion. Then I asked him if he believed he was created in God's image, and he replied in the affirmative. I said, "If you are God's image, you are exactly like Him; He has to have a bunion before you can get one, and that is an utter impossibility."

The healing was instantaneous and he has never had a return of the trouble. This demonstration was made by proving the truth about God so conclusively that the opposite seemed ridiculous. It certainly is ridiculous to think of God manifesting bunions.

*To Change Your
Body, Change Your Thought*

The practitioner does not change the bodily condition of his patient. He changes the patient's thought from erring belief to truth; then the patient's mind objectifies the changed thoughts upon his body or in his circumstances.

The one essential truth is that there is nothing for us to do but make the proper thought conditions through which Mind can reveal the kingdom here and now.

God's creation is finished. This creation is being revealed through the mind of man. As Life continues to unfold, express, or objectify Itself, we see this objective state in tangible form.

Working out your problems from this finished basis makes demonstrating a certainty rather than a game of chance. A demonstration is a revelation to the consciousness of that which already is in heaven.

*Be Single-Minded
and You Will Be Healthy*

You must be careful not to be double-minded; that is, saying one thing when you mean another, or thinking the truth one moment and the opposite the next, thus neutralizing your thoughts.

St. James said, "A double-minded man is unstable in all his ways. Let not that man think that he shall receive anything of the Lord."

Your mind fulfills your prayers or desires and is the Lord spoken of by St. James. If the thoughts held in your mind are fluctuating between disease and health, poverty and wealth, your mind cannot teach a solid conviction, and therefore there can be no expression or demonstration until a conclusion is reached and held in mind.

Cease "asking" for things and begin to "take" that which God has created and given you. God freely offers every desirable thing. In order to receive, you must mentally accept it (believe that you have it). Mentally claim health, happiness, and success.

If you are ill, you continually claim you are ill—thereby you accept (claim) it, and diseased thoughts continue to manifest a diseased body. Reverse the process and you will manifest health.

Fulfillment precedes the demand. Desire is an indication that the thing desired is awaiting your acceptance.

I had a very marked proof of this one year when I was preparing for a trip to Alaska. In taking stock to see what articles I needed for my journey, I became conscious of a desire for face powder and perfume. Knowing that to contemplate desire would be to admit a lack of these articles, I reversed my thoughts in this manner:

> There is no desire in heaven—spiritual man is instantly in possession of everything he needs. I am not body—I am mind. Perfume and powder are infinite ideas, tangible and real to spiritual consciousness. When my mind becomes conscious of perfume and powder, I have received the very things. I thank thee, Father, for my perfume and powder.

I went on packing my trunk, thoroughly satisfied I had received. In less than fifteen minutes, a friend came to bid me goodbye. She brought me face powder and perfume as a gift for my journey. Jesus said, "Whatsoever things ye desire, believe ye have received them."

Why Many Fail to Demonstrate

Most people fail to demonstrate because they believe they are body rather than Mind. Believe you are mental (spiritual) beings, and you will soon realize that your ideas are your realities. "The things (ideas) which are unseen are eternal." I mentally claimed my perfume and powder, and they were made manifest through a channel deducted by Mind.

You must not outline how God will reveal His creation to you—that is His business. You know what you want; accept it in its fullness and completeness—know how you would feel in possession of the thing desired, and leave it to Him.

Chapter VII

Healing Disease and Mental Diagnosis

"Wisdom is the principal thing; therefore get wisdom; and with all they getting get understanding" (Solomon, Prov. 4:7).

We all have problems to meet, and there are times when a case is slow in responding to treatment. This is the time to use wisdom and uncover the seeming cause that is manifesting the apparent condition upon the body or in your affairs.

Knowing that everything in the visible world is the objective state of a belief held in mind, it is quite evident that by close observation of the visible manifestation it is quite easy to determine the thoughts you have to deal with. St. Paul said, "The things which are not seen are clearly discerned by the things which are seen."

The mentality always has an objective side, so your body and affairs may be termed the objective state of your mentality which is called "you." Mentality and the body coexist as cause and effect.

Every creation or idea of Spirit has its symbol in some material belief. For every object in this universe, there is the existence of a spiritual reality in mind.

In healing, it is often beneficial to know the spiritual realities of the body. Space will not permit me to give you a list of them, but they are to be found in *Life Understood* or *Treatment* by F. L. Rawson.

Mental Resistance Leads to Indigestion

Once we know what idea each bodily organ expresses, it is easy to read from symptoms expressed by certain organs just what beliefs the patient is holding in mind. To remove the effect, you must first destroy the false beliefs in the mentality by knowing the truth. This is not always necessary for an advanced worker, but it is of great help to a student who is not able to heal by a realization of the nothingness of evil and the Allness of God.

For example, I had a man come to me who was suffering from indigestion. Everything he ate set up fermentation. I knew the stomach symbolized Intelligence, Mind. He was a person who would not accept an idea without reasoning, arguing, and nine times out of ten refused to accept any ideas without actual demonstration.

Food symbolizes God's ideas that nourish man. That which went on in his mentality was out-pictured in his stomach, which in turn symbolizes Intelligence. Instead of acting like any intelligent person should act, by accepting ideas that were presented to him, digesting, assimilating and passing them on, he always set up an argument against them. As soon as he began to give food to his stomach, it also refused to accept, digest, assimilate, or pass it on. I did not treat indigestion—I pointed out the error in his reasoning, and he was healed.

Arthritis the Result of Cramped Thoughts

A woman came to me suffering from arthritis. When I saw her cramped-up body, I knew that she was entertaining cramped-up thoughts, so I asked her what she was resenting. She was surprised that I could thus seemingly read her thoughts. I discovered her sister had died and left her money to someone else, and she could not let go of her resentment. When I told her what was causing arthritis, she was disappointed and informed me that she could never forgive her sister. I could do nothing for her as long as she nursed resentment.

I knew a lady who was drowned in a shipwreck. The mental shock her sister received upon hearing of the tragedy caused heart trouble, high blood pressure, and a nervous breakdown. The case came to me for treatment. I knew her bodily suffering was the effect of a material picture of a shipwreck held in mind. I denied that Mind, God, could ever be shocked. I knew her heart symbolized Love, and Love is God, therefore Love could never be affected by a mental shock. I realized the ship was a perfect idea in Mind and no ideas are lost—her sister's life is God and therefore never died. Working in this way for unity of thought, the false picture was destroyed, and she was healed in five days.

Hatred Creates Liver Trouble

Thoughts of hatred cause excessive bile and upset the liver. Patience is the remedy for liver trouble. The liver separates bile from the blood as patience separates you from thoughts of hatred. If you are not impatient, you will never have a feeling of hatred.

Anger causes you to reason wrongly, and uncontrolled reason brings on indigestion. Hurry, worry, trying to cram two days into one, violates Nature's laws, for Nature is always calm. This habit will cause neuritis. Hurry and worry bring on fear, and fear causes inflammation. Neuritis is inflammation of the nerves. The remedy is to cultivate peace and poise.

Criticism and Poverty

Criticism will block your supply. Criticism is seeing lack, not only in people but in everything you criticize. Your supply is a rich consciousness; criticism indicates that you are seeing the opposite, and if you continue this practice, you will manifest lack in your own affairs.

Never feel sorry for others or sympathize with error. When others tell you of error, mentally see beyond it, reverse your thoughts as they speak, and you will not only heal them but protect yourself.

Sometimes a disease is brought on by the patient's fear of it. As Job said, "The thing which I greatly feared has come upon me."

I met a woman who had a tumor, the result of fear entertained for thirty years while nursing an aunt with the same malady. In this case, the fear must be treated instead of the growth.

Kidney trouble is either the outpicturing of the lack of discrimination or the manifestation of the fear of it. A determined effort to discriminate between right and wrong will heal it.

Lung Trouble Signifies Mental Stagnation

Lung trouble is usually caused by mental suffocation. By this I mean a lack of opportunity to gather new inspiration, new hopes, new animation. The lungs symbolize Life, and when one's life lacks the environment, inspiration, and comfort needed, the mentality droops and becomes hopeless. This images on the body as tuberculosis. A change of climate, scenery, and environment gives the mind new inspiration and life, and these thoughts out-picture as new lung tissue.

Constipation is caused by stubborn thoughts. Stubbornness denotes an inability to give way in mind. The bowels symbolize channels in consciousness. If these thought channels are blocked by stubbornness, the bowels will manifest the same condition. Learn to give freely, and you will be healed.

People who always feel cold fail to express love. Cultivate an interest in life, and you will have perfect circulation of blood. Bloods symbolizes joy—if you lack joy, stir up new ambitions.

*Eyes Healed through Faith
in the Power of Sight*

A woman asked me to treat for her eyes so that she could put off glasses she had worn for many years. I explained that glasses had no power to improve her eyesight and that when she put glasses on she merely saw through her "belief" in them. I explained that if she believed she could see without the glasses, her mind would manifest that belief. Her enlightened consciousness gave her the vision she desired, and she was healed the next day. I saw her four years later, and she had never again worn glasses.

A similar healing occurred in connection with a young woman using crutches. As I looked at her crutches leaning against the wall, I called her attention to the fact that they could not hold themselves up and asked her how she could rely upon them for support. I explained how her mind believed they supported her but that it was God's idea of support that held her up. She laughed, caught the vision, and within six hours was healed. "With all they getting, get understanding."

As you advance in understanding, you will be able to discern error intuitively. To understand that Mind is infinite, not dependent upon the physical senses, is a step towards the Mind-science by which we discern man's existence and nature.

Seeing Error Makes It Possible to Destroy It

When we have thoroughly learned and digested this mental science, we can know all things past, present, and future. This Mind-reading is not clairvoyance. It is the illumination of the Soul-sense which comes to the human mind when the latter yields to the divine Mind, God. One metaphysician wrote:

> You will reach the perfect Science of healing when able to read the human mind after this manner, and discern the error you would destroy *(Science and Health)*.

Jesus journeyed with his students and "knew their thoughts"—read them scientifically. In like manner he discerned disease and healed the sick. He rebuked the lack of this power when he said, "O ye hypocrites! Ye can discern the face of the sky; but can ye not discern the signs of the times?"

Chapter VIII

How to Realize Prosperity

This lesson is written for the purpose of helping the student to demonstrate supply.

First of all, what do you call your supply? If you consider yourself a material man, you are then dependent upon material money and the things of this world for your substance, and the world belief is that they are hard to get; that you cannot be clothed, fed, or cared for without money. Yet Jesus said:

> Consider the lilies of the field, how they grow; they toil not, neither do they spin: And yet I say unto you, that Solomon in all his glory was not arrayed like one of these.

Solomon was the richest man of his day, and yet his advice to mankind was to gain understanding. In the book of Proverbs, we read these words:

> Happy is the man that findeth wisdom, and the man that getteth understanding, for the merchandise of it is better than the merchandise of silver, and the gain thereof than fine gold. She is more precious than rubies: and all the things thou canst desire are not to be compared unto her.

The True Source of Wealth

Solomon was leaning upon the substance of the unseen ideas in mind which are eternal, whereas the objects we behold with the five physical senses are but symbols and are perishable.

In this day of scientific understanding, we know that man is not material, so we will assume the spiritual man and reason from that basis.

God, Substance, Life, Mind, Consciousness, are all synonymous terms for the One Supreme Being. Understanding can give us more than gold or silver, for understanding is spiritual consciousness which is substance; whereas, gold and silver are but symbols or objects bearing evidence to the omnipresence of substance. Depending upon anything in manifestation is a dependence upon man (manifestation) instead of God, Substance.

Jesus performed miracles through understanding his own mind. This understanding endowed him with the Christ-Consciousness, which is the power of God. He never went outside of himself for any assistance. His understanding was the "substance of things hoped for." He did not have to accumulate and store up for the future, for his understanding of the nature of his own mind was an instantaneous source of supply.

There is no distance between the idea of the thing you desire and the mind that supplies it, for the idea is in mind. This is what Jesus meant when he said, "Whatsoever things ye desire, believe that ye have received them." God has nothing to give you but ideas, and these ideas are your sustenance and support, for you are a spiritual (mental) being; therefore, nothing can nourish you but God's ideas. Since you are mind and not body, the consciousness of an idea is equivalent to receiving the thing itself, for all God's ideas are things in reality.

The average person lives in the outer world, instead of the inner kingdom which is within his own consciousness. By so doing, the objects of sense seem to be realities, and he has depended upon them for so long that he is afraid to release them in thought for fear he will lose them. Yet Jesus said, "Whosoever will lose his life for my sake shall find it." When you lose your life for his sake, you have simply lost the false sense of a material man and have gained an understanding of your real Self as the spiritual man, the Christ-Consciousness of God. Finding this understanding of your true Self is finding your life "hid with Christ (in true consciousness) in God."

To Demonstrate Money

In order to demonstrate money, you must see it as a manifestation but not as reality. You cannot separate money as an idea from the Mind, God, but you must learn that it is the idea that sustains and supports. Once you see this clearly, you will appreciate Solomon's advice to get understanding.

In heaven, the world of reality, there are no solid objects such as money, houses, lands, etc. These objects are all in the world of creation. They are called creation because they have a beginning and end. It is perfectly right that we have all of these things we desire, and we possess them just as soon as we realize that the things in this world are but dream-pictures and that their existence is dependent upon the ideas of joy, happiness, and satisfaction that these symbols stand for in the world of reality. As soon as you see that an object in this world is but a shadow of a spiritual image or idea in mind, you will depend upon your ideas for supply rather than the things of this world. And when your mind furnishes you with ideas, do not sit down and wait for God to carry them out, but act upon your ideas. Thus, your ideas in mind become your supply.

You Must Act to Demonstrate

The world is full of people waiting upon God and wondering why they do not demonstrate. *Man is God's activity, and the more active you are the more you represent your true Self.*

Insight or understanding is the only means of deliverance. Until one gains the true viewpoint of the material world, he will continue to lack and will spend his days trying to demonstrate. Once you perceive the Allness of the spiritual creation and the nothingness of the material creation, your supply will come as naturally as the lily's, without anxious thought.

The only true creation is spiritual consciousness. Things do not come *out* of it—they are eternally within it. By understanding this, our ideas seem to be objectified or flashed before us as objects, just as moving pictures are flashed on the screen, but they really never leave the projection room.

This material creation is like a mirror—a vast infinite nothing. A mirror is really nothing, yet out of the mirror anything can spring. Any object placed before the mirror will be seen as a reflection. Suppose I held a gold coin up in front of a mirror; the coin would instantly be reflected back to me. The coin doesn't get into the mirror—it is merely seen as a reflection. The coin held before the mirror represents the idea held in spiritual consciousness. Held in consciousness, it *seems* to be projected, reflected, or objectified, but in reality it is eternally poised in the same place in Mind.

Depending upon money or any other thing in this world for your support or supply is equivalent to depending upon the reflection of the gold coin in the mirror instead of the original held before the mirror. It is quite evident that the coin in the mirror is nothing at all; therefore, a reliance upon it for supply is futile.

How to Realize Prosperity

Your Thoughts Determine What You Demonstrate

Once you realize that the kingdom of heaven is within you, you will see that the manifest world is no more substantial than the pictures on the screen. They appear to be so real to you that before you are aware of it you have made yourself so at one with the picture that you suffer or enjoy according to what your eyes behold. And yet there is nothing before you but a very dark, blank curtain. All action is taking place in the projection room.

Experiences of lack are but false pictures in your own mentality being flashed before your five physical senses, having no more reality than the pictures on the screen.

Suppose someone turned a bright light upon the screen while the picture was being shown. What would become of the picture or creation? It would be totally absorbed by the light. So it is with lack. By turning on the full light of understanding that now you are a spiritual being in possession of all the wealth of the kingdom, the false belief of lack is totally absorbed by the light of spiritual understanding being projected by the camera of divine Mind, and the false picture vanishes into its native nothingness.

Wealth is an established fact, and you can have as much as you can realize. The question naturally arises, "How am I to demonstrate the things I desire?" Get a definite idea of the thing you desire and hold to it unwaveringly. Do not outline the channel through which you think it should come.

For example, you may desire a car. If you believe that your possession of a car depends on money, your car will be limited to that one channel of supply, and if the money is not forthcoming, you do not demonstrate the car. But if you arouse the spiritual consciousness of joy, satisfaction, and appreciation that naturally accompanies the fulfillment of your desire for a car, you will soon possess it.

Many believe if they can demonstrate things their happiness will follow, but happiness is not the result of possessing things. Things are a result of happiness within your consciousness. Jesus distinctly said, "Seek ye first the kingdom ... and all things shall be added."

Chapter IX

How to See Yourself in Truth

There is one thing you must clearly understand if you desire to heal disease or any discordant condition: *Truth is all there is; therefore, evil is nothing.* Since evil is *nothing*, you do not have to struggle to be free, but you must understand that *in Truth you are eternally free*.

This understanding of the Truth dispels the illusion of the senses, and you witness health in place of disease, wealth in place of poverty, harmony in place of discord. This transformation is commonly called a healing.

The human mind is always creating pictures or images, in the same manner as you create men, women, and experiences in your sleeping dream. These pictures are thoughts, for you really think in pictures. The life, love, wisdom, beauty, joy, health and happiness that you see in this world is reality, heaven, and can never be lost or destroyed.

But sin, sickness, poverty, jealousy, crime, etc., are the false pictures that have no more life or permanence than the cinema pictures and can be caused to disappear as readily.

The Healing Truth You Want to Know

*Your Thoughts Are
Flashed Like a Picture Film*

Thoughts flash before your consciousness identically the same as the picture film is flashed before the light. The light gives life and animation to the pictures and projects them upon the screen. Your Mind or Consciousness stands in the same relationship to your thoughts as the light stands to the negatives or films. If you will not allow false thoughts to be held before the light of your own mind, it will be impossible for false conditions to become visible to you. It is impossible to show a moving picture unless the screen is in total darkness. It is just as impossible to project pictures of evil into your affairs unless your mind is in total darkness—that is, ignorant of the Truth.

Suppose you were witnessing a very sad scene in a picture and you did not desire to be affected by it. A realization of the fact that there was nothing before your eyes but a blank screen, and that all action was illusion, would instantly release you from any unpleasantness. Thus, "the truth would make you free."

Now suppose you were witnessing or experiencing disease, poverty, domestic difficulties, or business worries in your own life and desired to be free—you would release yourself in the same manner.

How to See Yourself in Truth

*You Cannot Heal Disease by
Turning Away from It*

You cannot heal disease or any inharmonious condition by simply turning your back on it or by declaring it is not there—it is an understanding of *why* it is impossible for God's man to experience anything but good that breaks the yoke of bondage and sets you free.

To realize that the seeming evil conditions are illusions or pictures projected by a false mentality, having no relationship to you, is to experience absolute freedom. You do not have to remove the picture from the screen to be free from it—you only have to know that it is not there in reality.

Through this explanation of the illusory nature of evil, it is quite evident that the only power evil has is to destroy itself. Turning the lie of error back upon itself is error's self-destruction. As it is impossible to project a photo play upon a brightly illumined screen, so it is just as impossible to manifest or project evil upon your screen of life when your consciousness is illumined by the Light of Truth.

An Important Point in Demonstrating

One important point to be considered in demonstrating is this: you must not be concerned about demonstrating *things*, but always bear in mind that your sole purpose is to demonstrate the Principle of your being. Jesus did not exploit himself, but his mission on earth was for the purpose of revealing to mankind the underlying principle of reality and to prove that heaven is here and now. He fulfilled the Law.

To a child or one who has little or no understanding of the principle of mathematics, the numerals are of no avail, yet the answer to every problem is just as available to him as to an expert mathematician. The only difference between the child and the expert is one of understanding.

So it is in working out problems of life. The one who understands his divine nature, his underlying Principle, will not be alarmed and dismayed by every problem. His understanding of Truth will be the illumination that causes illusions and deceptions to vanish. "Before they call, I will answer" means that before you even begin to wonder how your problem will be solved, the answer is already established in the kingdom of heaven, governed and controlled by the principle of perfection. God's creation is finished; you have only to avail yourself of the principles in order to enjoy all the luxuries of heaven just at hand.

There Is a Perfect Law of Supply and Demand

There is a perfect law of supply and demand, desire and fulfilment. You cannot possibly desire a thing that has not already been fulfilled.

You adjust your radio to the wavelength that connects you with certain stations if you wish to enjoy the program. You do not bring the program to you, but you "tune in" to that which is instantly available.

*Adjust Your Mental Radio
and Demonstrations Will Come*

Demonstrations will come to you as readily as harmony comes to your radio when you learn to adjust your "mental radio" and "tune in" to heaven, which surrounds you at this very instant. God, the only Cause and Creator of all good, is broadcasting from the station of heaven on an infinite wavelength of Love. Turn the dials of your mental radio away from the static of materiality and "listen in" on harmony.

Be aware at this very instant that perfect health, prosperity, success, abundance, perfect adjustment, are eternally present, existing like the wavelength, right where you are.

Tune out discord; listen in on harmony. Be receptive; accept the kingdom as an established fact, the only true broadcasting station; nothing to be changed, nothing to be destroyed, nothing to be healed—*just something to understand*.

This is the message of Absolute Truth, the kingdom of heaven at hand.

Chapter X

The Basis of Healing

The principal thing in treatment is to take your thought off your patient, his troubles and the material world, and to actively, consciously think of God and heaven.

The greater your knowledge of the world of reality the easier it is to heal, for this tends to greater mental activity and a better elimination of material thoughts.

When you treat, you should not take the attitude that you are trying to bring about a demonstration, *for this implies a belief in some evil to be overcome.*

Let your treatment be an attitude of loyalty to God. You treat because it is right for you to bear witness to the Truth. Thinking of God and heaven prevents evil thoughts from entering your mind, for you cannot think of good and evil at the same time.

St. Paul said, "Henceforth know we no man after the flesh" (2 Cor. 5:16). In other words, we are not to recognize our fellow man as a material being subject to sin, disease, and death, but we are to behold him as a spiritual being, reflecting all the powers and aspects of God.

The realization and affirmation of God's perfect world should be dwelt upon throughout the day as much as possible. Our progress depends on how consistently we watch our thoughts throughout the twenty-four hours, reversing every thought which is unlike God and His perfect world. This is "dwelling in the secret place of the most High."

We must learn to wield the two-edged sword of Truth by the continual use of the denial and affirmation. These are known throughout the Bible as the rod and the staff, the greater light and the lesser light, as rebuke and chasten.

Jesus said, "Let your communication be, Yea, yea; Nay, nay: for whatsoever is more than these cometh of evil" (Matt. 5:37). Yea, yea, is the affirmation, and Nay, nay, is the denial.

How to Pray

Jesus said, "If any man will come after me, let him deny himself, and take up his cross daily, and follow me" (Luke 9:23).

This means that you must deny the reality of matter, take up in thought—true prayer—your problems one by one, and follow Jesus in thought to God and heaven.

Commence your treatment by forming as clear a concept of God as possible. It does not matter what your concept is so long as it is your highest realization of good.

Some find it a great help to realize God in His various aspects of Love, Life, and Truth, Soul, Spirit, Intelligence, Principle, the Principle of all law and order. I find that a realization of God as a vast, infinite Mind wherein dwell all of God's spiritual beings (ideas), by means of which Mind thinks and acts, gives me the greatest mental activity.

Wherever Mind is, Consciousness is. That Consciousness is the Christ, or man specifically; that is, all the spiritual beings in heaven. Paul called this consciousness "Christ the power of God, and the wisdom of God" (1 Cor. 1:24).

While you are thinking of God and His perfect world, deny the existence in heaven of the particular trouble you wish to overcome. Use one denial, but let it be clear and decisive. Follow the denial immediately with as many affirmations as possible, dwelling upon the exact opposite of the evil that you have denied.

For instance, if you were treating against anger, turn in thought to God and heaven and realize: "There is no anger (in heaven); all is infinite Love. Man is God's consciousness; therefore, he reflects Love and is loving towards all." Then dwell upon Love as long as possible.

If you do your work impersonally, striving to realize the perfection of God and His perfect world, and do not doubt the action of God, you will make your demonstrations. Do not attempt to follow any fixed formula or rules, but let God lead you. The power is not in the words you use but in the realization of the underlying principle. You will find that the constant reversal of thought is an easy, scientific, and therefore sure way of getting rid of troubles for yourself and others.

The following treatments for specific problems will give you an idea of how to reverse your thoughts.

Want of Joy

There is no want of joy (in heaven), for man is the joyous activity of God. Man is always receiving joyous ideas from God, Mind, and he passes on these ideas to his fellow man, giving him joy and happiness, thus receiving infinite joy and happiness in turn.

Nothing can prevent this joyous activity, for there is but one power, God, and man is governed and controlled by God alone. "In thy presence is fullness of joy; at thy right hand there are pleasures for evermore" (Ps. 16:11).

Unemployment

Man is never out of work, for man is the activity of God. Man is the consciousness of God, and Mind is eternally unfolding infinite ideas which radiate out in consciousness, giving man infinite activity. Man rejoices in receiving God's ideas and expressing them, always reflecting Love.

Man is never idle, for when man works, God works, for God works by means of man. Not one of God's ideas is ever idle; each has its special purpose. When God thinks, His ideas move, and this movement is man.

There is a perfect law of supply and demand; when man needs an idea, he is instantly in touch with it, for Mind and Its ideas are never separated. Man is God's consciousness, and Mind is always at work; therefore, man and his work are never separated.

When you have treated in this manner, then take the necessary steps in following the ideas that have come to your consciousness relative to the securing of a position, and rely upon the action of God (treatment) to adjust the matter satisfactorily.

Fear

There is no fear. Man has absolute trust in God, in good. Man, being God's consciousness, is eternally poised in Mind and absolutely fearless. No thoughts of fear can touch man, for he is surrounded by infinite peace and love, and only God's thoughts can come to man. (Fear, properly utilized, is a signpost on the way to heaven—it is a signal to reverse your thoughts and avoid danger.)

Jealousy

When thoughts of jealousy attack you or those around you, turn in thought to heaven and realize the infinite love, appreciation, and understanding of God. Realize that man is always helping and benefiting his fellow man.

Sin

To heal sin, reverse the thoughts by dwelling upon the purity and holiness of man in God's image. Strive to realize how impossible it is for God's man to violate a law, for all laws are God's laws. God is the principle of all law and order. There is no material man to sin, only God's spiritual man. When man acts, God acts; therefore all activity is perfect, reflecting God's purity and holiness. "Whosoever is born of God doth not commit sin" (1 John 3:9).

Anxiety

One becomes anxious and fearful because he does not realize that he is governed and controlled by God. Thoughts of anxiety are reversed by realizing the absolute confidence that your spiritual Self has in the certainty of God's action. There are no cares in the spiritual world, for God is the only thinker. No false thoughts to come to man's consciousness, for only God's ideas of joy, happiness, and freedom unfold to man. The action of Truth is always producing harmony.

Sale of Property

Everything in the so-called material world is a symbol, bearing evidence to unseen ideas in Mind.

For instance, property of any description represents certain combinations of ideas which have come to your consciousness. When you desire to sell something, it is your spiritual Self passing on ideas to your fellow man in the world of reality. To overcome the various beliefs in this world associated with buying or selling, you must reverse this seeming action and realize what is going on in heaven.

In heaven, there is a perfect law of supply and demand. For instance, when man desires to pass on (sell) an idea (property), he knows where to pass it, for God is the Principle of all knowledge. Love is the power which causes man to pass on the ideas, and Love causes your fellow man to want to receive (appears as buying) your ideas.

This activity of buying and selling is man's perfect work, reflecting divine wisdom, knowledge, and intelligence.

I was asked to give a treatment for the sale of a lot, and I reversed my thoughts in this manner. The following morning, the woman who owned the lot phoned me. She said a gentleman whom she did not know had phoned and wanted to buy her lot. She could not understand how it happened or how he knew she had a lot to sell.

Mind is in touch with all of Its ideas, whether they are houses, lots, or men and women. Heaven is the place where God works, so if you desire to witness perfect work in this world, you must first do your mental work in heaven. Houses and lots must first be sold in heaven. Many people try to sell property while they still insist upon holding to

The Basis of Healing

it mentally. If you desire to be free from anything (disease included), you must *release* it in mind.

Right Place

Sometimes one feels he is not in his right place; that his work is unsatisfactory and yet he is unable to adjust himself. For this condition, turn away from the material appearance and treat in this manner: There is no indecision; God rules and governs man. Man is always in his right place in Mind.

Man never has inferior work; man's work is perfect, for man is spiritual, divine. There is no mortal power to keep a man out of his right place, for man is as infinite as God is infinite. Man works in the presence of God, receiving and passing on the glorious ideas of God which radiate out in consciousness, giving man infinite joy and happiness. Man's work is never unremunerative; man receives just return for every idea he gives, for God is the source of all supply.

Taking Material Steps

There is a great deal of misapprehension among Truth students in regard to taking "material steps" while working out problems in the light of spiritual understanding. The most essential thing to be considered in Absolute Science is the practical application of Truth principles. This application does not consist in doing your daily lesson, studying courses in mental science, tithing a certain portion, attending regular meetings, and the remainder of your time waiting for something to happen. If you are applying your principles, you are *acting* as though you possess the intelligence and power of God.

Jesus Christ not only spoke the word of Truth, but he was an actual doer—he was both mentally and physically *active*. The principle of mathematics contains natural rules and laws which, when applied, bring about natural results. The principle of life is the same; and one of its laws is action.

Man is the activity of God, and the more truth you know about yourself the more active you will become. This does not necessarily imply that your activity will be physical or laborious, but you must be active in order to express God. If you find yourself doing physical labor, by knowing the truth that man is the activity of God your labor will be joyous and will not fatigue you.

When you have faith that you are a spiritual being in heaven here and now, you will not hesitate in taking action.

There is no material activity; all action is God's action—spiritual, perfect, and divine.

Supply

People often wonder why they do not demonstrate supply, but they never ask themselves, "What am I contributing to the world to deserve remuneration?"

"Give, and it shall be given unto you." You may say, "I can't give; I have no money." Money is not your supply; service is your supply. Jesus demonstrated that.

There is a vast difference between serving and rendering a service. You may labor very hard *serving* someone, but true service consists in a benefit or advantage conferred upon an individual or the world in general. The person who conceives right ideas and puts them into action renders a service and receives supply in direct proportion.

Man's true supply is a wealth of ideas; therefore, when you are treating for supply, you are actually endeavoring to become conscious of the infinite ideas available to Mind at this instant.

Henry Ford demonstrated abundant supply by getting the idea of putting an inexpensive car on the market. This idea has rendered service to humanity in general and has given infinite joy and happiness. In turn, Mr. Ford has received compensation for his *activity*, in terms of what we call money.

About the Author

Vivian May Williams was an independent lecturer from coast to coast and was a teacher and practitioner of Absolute Truth for many years.

She was an editor of *Freedom Magazine*, which presented the message of Absolute Truth, and contributed articles to *Psychology Magazine* and *Nautilus Magazine*, which were an inspiration and guidance to thousands.

Asked to indicate the sources of her wide and deep understanding, she credited the vast silences and wide reading of the world's best teachers and a mastery of the new discoveries of science. This, combined with the inner illumination of her own spirit, contributed to make her message worthy of the most serious attention of all thoughtful and earnest souls.

www.ingramcontent.com/pod-product-compliance
Lightning Source LLC
Chambersburg PA
CBHW020019050426
42450CB00005B/553